D0984004

# TOP 10 WORST

# EARTHQUAKES

**Louise and Richard Spilsbury**

**PowerKiDS**
press
New York

Published in 2017 by
**The Rosen Publishing Group, Inc.**
29 East 21st Street, New York, NY 10010

Cataloging-in-Publication Data

Names: Spilsbury, Louise.
Title: Top 10 worst earthquakes / Louise and Richard Spilsbury.
Description: New York : PowerKids Press, 2017. | Series: Nature's ultimate disasters | Includes index.
Identifiers: ISBN 9781499430660 (pbk.) | ISBN 9781508153160 (library bound) | ISBN 9781499430677 (6 pack)
Subjects: LCSH: Earthquakes--Juvenile literature.
Classification: LCC QE521.3 S65 2017 | DDC 363.34'95--dc23

Copyright © 2017 by The Rosen Publishing Group

Produced for Rosen by Calcium
Editors for Calcium Creative Ltd: Sarah Eason and Harriet McGregor
Designers: Paul Myerscough and Simon Borrough
Picture research: Rachel Blount

Picture credits: Cover: Shutterstock: Petrafler (top), Somjin Klong-ugkara (bottom); Inside: NOAA: NGDC, M. Mehrain, Dames and Moore 13t; Shutterstock: Tracy Ben 19, Marisa Estivill 6–7, Everett Historical 21, Fotos593 4–5, Igor Golovniov 23, Junrong 25t, 25b, Shawn Kashou 17, Somjin Klong-ugkara 1, 11; Wikimedia Commons: UN Photo/Logan Abassi United Nations Development Programme 27, Arnold Genthe, Library of Congress 9, NOAA 7r, Uwebart 14–15.

Manufactured in the United States of America

CPSIA Compliance Information: Batch #BW17PK: For Further Information contact Rosen Publishing, New York, New York at 1-800-237-9932.

# Contents

# EARTHQUAKE DANGER

Earthquakes are natural events that can cause deadly disasters. In an earthquake, Earth's surface moves and trembles. The solid ground beneath buildings, roads, and homes shakes and can break open huge cracks in the land.

This road in Ecuador was cracked open on April 18, 2016, after a 7.8 **magnitude** earthquake.

## How Dangerous?

Some earthquakes are small. People may hardly notice that they happen or they may simply see a lamp swing slightly on the ceiling or a glass gently shake on a table. Some earthquakes are huge. As the ground moves, whole buildings can **collapse** and the air fills with a sound like a jet plane roaring past. Earthquakes can cause more damage than any other type of natural disaster.

# Measuring Disaster

When an earthquake happens, the ground shakes and moves.

→ **Seismologists** use **seismometers** to measure how much the ground shakes.

Small changes in Earth's **crust** can happen before an earthquake.

→ Seismologists study images taken by **satellites** to measure the shape of and changes to Earth's crust.

Scientists have devised the **Richter scale** to compare different earthquakes.

→ The Richter scale measures an earthquake by its strength, or magnitude. A magnitude 5.3 is a moderate earthquake. A 6.3 is a strong earthquake.

Natural disasters have taken place since Earth was formed. People have many ways of deciding what the world's worst natural disasters have been, from the deadliest disaster to the costliest. This book includes some of the worst disasters in history.

# EARTHQUAKES IN ACTION

How do earthquakes happen? Earth moves and shakes during a quake because of movements deep below its surface.

## Plates on the Move

Earth's crust is a layer of rock covering the surface of the planet. It consists of huge, rocky slabs that fit together like a jigsaw puzzle. These are called **tectonic plates**. The plates float like enormous rafts on hot, soft, and liquid rock called **magma** that lies deep inside Earth. The edges of the plates are called plate boundaries. The plates are constantly and very slowly moving around, sliding past and bumping into each other.

A rift valley is a long, deep crack in Earth's surface formed where the tectonic plates have moved apart.

## Faults

An earthquake happens when two of Earth's plates suddenly slip past one another. The weak area where two plates meet is called a **fault**. The edges of the plates are jagged and rough. As they push against each other, the **pressure** builds up until suddenly the two edges come apart and move past each other, causing an earthquake. The location directly above where the earthquake starts is called the **epicenter**. When the plates shift, they make the land all around them move too.

## A Powerful Quake

One of the most powerful earthquakes ever happened in Alaska, in 1964. It measured 9.2 on the Richter scale and was felt over a wide area. It caused a lot of damage and 131 people were killed. The reason so few lives were lost is that the quake happened in a place where not many people lived.

The 1964 Alaskan earthquake lasted 3 minutes, causing **landslides** and **tsunamis** that resulted in widespread damage.

# 10 SAN FRANCISCO

The earthquake that struck San Francisco, California, at 5:12 a.m. on the morning of April 18, 1906, was one of the worst natural disasters in the history of the United States. It was also one of the worst earthquakes of all time.

## The San Andreas Fault

## The San Andreas Fault

San Francisco lies on the San Andreas Fault. There had been quakes along this fault before, but this one cracked the ground along the fault line for about 300 miles (480 km). That is almost half the length of California. The earthquake shook the ground for a full minute. It toppled buildings and damaged fuel and power lines, which set off devastating fires.

# On the Record

Experts believe that the 1906 earthquake must have measured 7.8 on the Richter scale. It killed between 700 and 3,000 people.

The earthquake was one of the strongest ever felt in North America. The shock reached all the way from Coos Bay, Oregon, to Los Angeles, California, and as far east as central Nevada, an area of about 375,000 square miles (970,000 sq km).

The 1906 San Francisco earthquake was one of the world's first major natural disaster to be recorded in photographs.

The earthquake destroyed 28,000 buildings and left more than 225,000 of the city's 400,000 residents homeless.

Fires burned out of control for three days and nights. Some of the fires reached temperatures of 2,700 degrees Fahrenheit (1,480° C). The fires destroyed about one-quarter of the city.

# 9 NEPAL

On April 25, 2015, a massive earthquake struck Nepal between the capital city Kathmandu and the city of Pokhara, 125 miles (200 km) away. The disaster killed almost 9,000 people and injured thousands more. It also flattened or damaged over 850,000 homes, as well as schools, clinics, and other buildings.

**Nepal**

## Aftershocks

The earthquake measured 7.8 on the Richter scale. It was followed by dangerous **aftershocks**. Aftershocks are smaller earthquakes that happen a short time after a big earthquake in the same area as the main shock. As well as a large number of smaller aftershocks, there was also a very damaging one that measured 7.3, on May 12, 2015.

# On the Record

One of the worst-hit areas was Sindhupalchok. More than 2,000 people died in this district alone. In Kathmandu, over 1,000 people lost their lives.

Thousands of people were killed or badly injured when they were hit by collapsing buildings or by falling **debris**. Mount Everest was also struck by deadly **avalanches** caused by the quake on April 25.

The earthquake destroyed many buildings in Kavreplanchok district, Nepal.

After the earthquakes, many people slept in tents and shelters around Kathmandu for weeks. Some people had lost their homes, but others were too afraid to sleep in buildings in case there were more aftershocks.

This was the worst earthquake to hit Nepal for 80 years. The disaster affected more than 8 million people, many living in **remote** and mountainous areas of the country.

# 8 IRAN

At 12:30 a.m. on June 21, 1990, while most people were sleeping, there was a magnitude 7.7 earthquake along the shores of the Caspian Sea in northern Iran. It brought terrible destruction to the region. Many homes were built simply and could not withstand the quake and the aftershocks that followed.

**Iran**

## Shaking Soils

The earthquake's epicenter was very close to the surface so it was very destructive. The land in this area consists of large amounts of sand and mud, which shakes a lot more than hard rock, causing greater damage. The earthquake also caused **liquefaction**. This is when the damp ground can no longer support the weight of buildings above. The buildings fall into the crumbling land beneath them.

# On the Record

The earthquake destroyed the cities of Rudbar, Manjil, and Lushan, and 700 villages. At least 300 other villages were also damaged.

An area of 20,000 square miles (50,000 sq km) was absolutely devastated.

The earthquake killed about 40,000 people and injured 60,000 more.

In this mountain village near Manjil, most buildings were made of dried mud and collapsed instantly during the quake.

Approximately 100,000 buildings collapsed or were damaged, leaving 500,000 people without homes.

During the dark night hours that followed the quake, it was difficult for help to reach remote mountain villages. Landslides and rubble blocked paths and roads, preventing ambulances and rescue vehicles from getting through.

# 7 PERU

At 3:20 p.m. on May 31, 1970, the deadliest earthquake South America has ever known shook Peru. The quake had a magnitude of 7.9. The epicenter was under the Pacific Ocean about 15 miles (25 km) west of the coastal town of Chimbote, in north-central Peru.

## Coastal Catastrophe

The most damage occurred in the coastal towns near the epicenter, but the effects of the quake were felt in the capital city of Lima, more than 400 miles (650 km) away. People were also killed by a series of landslides when the earthquake dislodged rock and ice at the tops of mountains. About 70,000 people were killed in the disaster and more than 800,000 were made homeless.

Peru

# On the Record

The earthquake lasted 45 seconds and damaged or destroyed roads, bridges, and buildings over an area of 32,000 square miles (83,000 sq km). This is an area bigger than Belgium and the Netherlands together!

Many of the homes and buildings in the area were made from **adobe**, a type of clay mud, and they were built on loose soil. Most people were killed or injured when their homes or businesses collapsed.

The worst landslide occurred on Mount Huascarán. A mass of snow, water, and mud sped down its side at up to 125 miles (200 km) per hour, devastating nearby towns and villages.

This picture shows the area that was covered by the landslide from Mount Huascarán.

The city of Yungay was filled with mud and debris up to 100 feet (30 m) deep by landslides.

# KASHMIR, PAKISTAN

## 6

The earthquake that struck the western Himalayan mountain region at 8:50 a.m. on October 8, 2005, had devastating results. Its epicenter was just 12 miles (19 km) northeast of Muzaffarabad city and district in Kashmir, and 65 miles (105 km) away from Islamabad, the capital of Pakistan.

Kashmir, Pakistan

### Far-Reaching Tremors

The earthquake's magnitude was 7.6 and the Muzaffarabad district was worst hit. The quake also caused major damage in northern Pakistan, northern India, and Afghanistan. The **tremors** were felt 620 miles (1,000 km) away in Delhi, the capital city of India.

# On the Record

The 2005 Kashmir earthquake actually made a crack in the planet's surface that **geologists** call a **surface rupture**. In some places, the earthquake shifted the ground more than 16 feet (5 m).

The total number of people killed by the earthquake, its aftershocks, and the landslides it caused was around 86,000. More than 69,000 people were injured.

The earthquake made 4 million people homeless, forcing them to live in tents.

The quake destroyed entire villages, and over 32,000 homes collapsed in cities in Kashmir. Buildings were also destroyed and damaged in Pakistan.

Rescuers could not get through to many of the victims of the disaster because of aftershocks.

# 5 SICHUAN, CHINA

The magnitude 7.9 earthquake that struck the mountainous region of Sichuan in southwestern China on May 12, 2008, was devastating. The epicenter was 50 miles (80 km) from the major city Chengdu, and 12 miles (19 km) below the surface.

## Sichuan, China

## Awful Impacts

The earthquake was the strongest to strike China since 1950. Tremors were felt as far away as Shanghai, 1,000 miles (1,700 km) from the epicenter. The effects of the disaster were terrible, not just because of the strength of the quake but because the area was so densely **populated**. Many of the buildings were made from mud bricks and were unable to cope with the shaking.

# On the Record

More than 87,150 people were killed or declared missing. Over 5,000 children died when the schools they were in collapsed.

Most people died immediately after the earthquake tremors, but hundreds more died later, because rescuers could not reach them in their remote mountain homes and villages.

The earthquake destroyed 80 percent of all the buildings in the area.

Falling debris and collapsing buildings injured a staggering 375,000 people.

More than 1.5 million homes were destroyed and 4.8 million people were left homeless by the disaster.

# KANTŌ, JAPAN

**4**

The worst earthquake to strike Japan in the twentieth century is known as the Great Kantō earthquake. It happened at 12:00 p.m. on September 1, 1923. It was a huge magnitude 7.9 earthquake that devastated the region around the capital Tokyo and nearby port Yokohama. It caused terrible damage across the whole Kantō region.

**Kantō, Japan**

## Lunchtime Fires

The disaster was made worse by the fact it hit at lunchtime when workers, students, and families were sitting down to a cooked meal. Shaking from the quake caused considerable damage but the tremors also knocked over stoves, which started fires. These were whipped up by strong winds and spread rapidly through the cities.

# On the Record

The earthquake lasted between 4 and 10 minutes.

In Yokohama, 9 out of 10 homes were destroyed or damaged. In Tokyo, 350,000 homes were wiped out, leaving more than half of the city's inhabitants with no place to live.

It is thought that up to 140,000 people died in this disaster.

The fires caused by the Great Kantō earthquake swept through Yokohama and Tokyo, burning everything and everyone in their path.

The earthquake set off an enormous tsunami that reached 40 feet (12 m) high. The giant waves carried thousands of people into the sea and to their deaths.

The Great Kantō earthquake was so powerful that it not only damaged the base of a 93-ton (84 mt) bronze statue of Great Buddha at Kamakura, but people say it also made the statue move forward by about 2 feet (60 cm).

# 3 MESSINA, ITALY

On December 28, 1908, at approximately 5:20 a.m., the most destructive earthquake to ever hit Europe shook southern Italy. The cities of Messina and Reggio Calabria were worst hit, but the effects of the earthquake and the fires and tsunami that followed were felt in most of southern Italy's coastal towns.

**Messina, Italy**

## A Double Disaster

The 7.5 magnitude earthquake lasted for about 20 seconds. Its epicenter was in the Messina Strait, the narrow passage of water that separates the island of Sicily from Calabria on mainland Italy. Moments after the quake, a tsunami formed, crashing into dozens of cities along both coastlines. More than 80,000 people were killed in this double disaster.

# On the Record

The shaking of the ground by the earthquake destroyed or damaged almost all of the buildings in Messina and Reggio Calabria. It broke fuel pipes and caused widespread fires.

The tsunami that followed brought waves estimated to be 40 feet (12 m) high flooding onto the shores of northern Sicily and southern Calabria.

Most of southern Italy's cities were devastated by the earthquake.

Some experts believe that the tsunami may not have been caused directly by the quake but by an underwater landslide, which happened seconds after the shock.

In the days after the main earthquake, there were hundreds of smaller aftershocks. These brought down many of the remaining buildings and injured or killed those trying to help victims of the first quake.

ЗЕМЛЕТРЯСЕНІЕ ВЪ
МЕССИНА.

# 2 TANGSHAN, CHINA

The earthquake that hit Tangshan, China, on July 28, 1976, was one of the deadliest in the twentieth century. More than 242,000 people were killed in this quake and the aftershocks that followed.

**Tangshan, China**

## Massive Tremors

The epicenter of the main 7.5 magnitude earthquake was in the southern part of the industrial city of Tangshan, 70 miles (110 km) east of the capital, Beijing. There was also a huge 7.5 magnitude aftershock later the same day, 43 miles (70 km) away. As well as the high death toll, more than 700,000 people were injured.

# On the Record

This sculpture of the residents of Tangshan in 1976 commemorates the disaster.

The main quake lasted about 16 seconds. It made the deep sandy soil in the region behave like a liquid, so most of the buildings in the affected area collapsed.

The earthquake bent and buckled railroad lines and collapsed highway bridges.

More than 85 percent of the buildings in Tangshan were destroyed or badly damaged, and some buildings were damaged in cities as far away as Beijing.

The main earthquake struck at 3:42 a.m., when most people were at home in bed. Most of those killed died when the tremors made their **unreinforced** stonework homes collapse on top of them.

The large aftershock caused more death and damage and made it even harder for rescuers to help victims trapped under collapsed buildings.

# HAITI

**1**

The epicenter of the earthquake that hit Haiti at 4:53 p.m. on January 12, 2010, was just 15 miles (25 km) southwest of the capital city Port au Prince. This enormous disaster affected around 3 million people, one-third of the country's population, making it the worst disaster in recent history.

Haiti

## Shaking at the Surface

Haiti's worst quake in two centuries was a magnitude 7.0 and it happened just 8 miles (13 km) below the surface. The fact that the quake was shallow made the movement of land above it even worse. People felt the ground below their feet shake all across Haiti and the Dominican Republic and in Cuba, Jamaica, and Puerto Rico.

# On the Record

The main quake was shortly followed by two aftershocks of magnitudes 5.9 and 5.5. Over the following days, there were more aftershocks, including one of magnitude 5.9 on January 20.

The highest number of deaths occurred in the capital, where 2.8 million people lived, many in narrow streets and in buildings not equipped to cope with a quake.

About 220,000 people were killed by the earthquake and aftershocks, and more than 300,000 people were injured.

About 1 million people were left homeless by the catastrophe.

The earthquake destroyed 100,000 houses and badly damaged almost 200,000 more.

The quake left 670 million cubic feet (19 million cu m) of rubble and debris in Port au Prince.

# WHERE IN THE WORLD?

**This map shows the locations of the earthquakes featured in this book.**

San Francisco, California

ATLANTIC OCEAN

Read the case studies about Haiti, the number 1 earthquake in this book, and San Francisco, the number 10 earthquake. How do they differ?

Haiti

Peru

Why do you think it is important to study earthquakes that have happened in the past? How could this help to save lives and buildings today?

How does the time of day of an earthquake affect the number of deaths or injuries? How do earthquakes cause terrible fires?

Messina, Italy

Tangshan, China

Sichuan, China

Iran

Kantō, Japan

Kashmir, Pakistan

Nepal

INDIAN OCEAN

What facts can you find in this book to support the argument that many deaths in these natural disasters happened not just because of the earthquake, but also because buildings were not built strongly enough?

# GLOSSARY

**adobe** A kind of clay used as a building material.

**aftershocks** Smaller earthquakes that happen shortly after a big earthquake.

**avalanches** Masses of snow, ice, or rocks that fall rapidly down mountainsides.

**collapse** When something suddenly falls or gives way.

**crust** Earth's outer layer of solid rock.

**debris** Loose waste material.

**epicenter** Point on Earth's surface above the place where an earthquake started.

**fault** The place where two or more different tectonic plates meet.

**geologists** Scientists who study planet Earth and how it is made.

**landslides** The collapses of masses of earth or rock from a mountain or cliff.

**liquefaction** When the strength or stiffness of soil is reduced by the movement of the ground.

**magma** Hot, liquid rock below Earth's surface.

**magnitude** Size, particularly of an earthquake.

**populated** Inhabited or full of people. People that live in an area populate it.

**pressure** A pushing force.

**remote** Far from main centers of population.

**Richter scale** Scale that tells people how powerful an earthquake is.

**satellites** Objects in space that travel around Earth.

**seismologists** Scientists who study earthquakes.

**seismometers** Machines that measure the movement of the ground during a volcanic eruption or earthquake.

**surface rupture** When movement on a fault deep within Earth breaks through to the surface.

**tectonic plates** The giant pieces of rock that fit together like a jigsaw puzzle to form Earth's crust.

**tremors** The shaking of the ground.

**tsunamis** Huge waves.

**unreinforced** Something that does not have a strong construction.

# FURTHER READING

## Books

Baker, John R. *The World's Worst Earthquakes* (World's Worst Natural Disasters). North Mankato, MN: Capstone Press, 2016.

*Earthquakes and Volcanoes* (Collins Fascinating Facts). New York, NY: Collins, 2016.

Meister, Cari. *Earthquakes* (Disaster Zone). Minneapolis, MN: Jump!, 2015.

## Websites

Due to the changing nature of Internet links, PowerKids Press has developed an online list of websites related to the subject of this book. This site is updated regularly. Please use this link to access the list: **www.powerkidslinks.com/nud/earthquakes**

# INDEX